NO KIDDING!

ANIMAL
Jokes, Riddles, and Games

Clara Christopher

Crabtree Publishing Company
www.crabtreebooks.com

Crabtree Publishing Company
www.crabtreebooks.com

Author: Clara Christopher

Editorial Director: Ellen Rodger

Art Director: Rosie Gowsell Pattison

Editor: Petrice Custance

Proofreader: Janine Deschenes

Prepress technician: Margaret Amy Salter

Print and production coordinator: Katherine Berti

Production coordinated by
Plan B Book Packagers

Photographs:
Cover and title page: Tanya Stock/Shutterstock; p.2: Serg 64/
Shutterstock; p.3: Jumnong/Shutterstock; p.4: Javier Brosch/
Shutterstock; p.5 (UP): Bike Rider London/Shutterstock; p.5 (LO):
Oksana 2010/Shutterstock; p.5 (LO), FPWing/Shutterstock; p.6:
Tobik/Shutterstock; p.7 (MIDLE): CKE/Shutterstock; p.7 (MIDRT):
Ded Mazay/Shutterstock; p.7 (LO): Tabby Mittins/Shutterstock; p.8
(LOLE): Nataliya Taratunina/Shutterstock; p. 8(LOLE): Su Xingmin/
Shutterstock; p.8 (LORT): Teguh Mujiono/Shutterstock; p.9 (UP):
Everett Collection /Shutterstock; p.9 (LO): 3 Dalia/Shutterstock; p.10
(UP): J. Stone/Shutterstock; p.10 (LO): Ron Leishman/Shutterstock;
p.11 (UP): Willee Cole Photography/Shutterstock; p.11 (LO): Vmaster/
Shutterstock; p.12: Vitaly Titov & Maria Sidelnikova/Shutterstock; p.13
(MID): Eric Isselee/Shutterstock; p.13 (MID): Operation Shooting/
Shutterstock; p.14: Paola Canzonetta/Shutterstock; p.15 (UP): Vicente
Barcelo Varona/Shutterstock; p.16 (LE): Pics Byst/Shutterstock; p.16
(RT): Shock Factor.de/Shutterstock; p.17 (UP): Chicco Dodi FC/
Shutterstock; p.17 (LO): Julien Tromeur/Shutterstock; p.18: Milsi
Art/Shutterstock; p.19 (UP): Ilya Akinshin/Shutterstock; p.19 (LO):
David Andrew Larsen/Shutterstock; p.20; BluIz 60/Shutterstock; p.21
(UPLE): Christopher Elwell/Shutterstock; p.21 (UPRT): Studio Axai/
Shutterstock; p.22 (MID): Julie DeGuia/Shutterstock; p.22 (LO): Susan
Schmitz/Shutterstock; p.23 (UP): Dudarev Mikhail/Shutterstock;
p.23 (LO): Julien Tromeur/Shutterstock; p.24: Andrey Makurin/
Shutterstock; p.25 (UP): Cool Kengzz/Shutterstock; p.25 (LO): Javier
Brosch/Shutterstock; p.26: Phy Zick/Shutterstock; p.27: Kenny K./
Shutterstock; p.29 (UP): Vitaly Titov & Maria Sidelnikova/Shutterstock;
p.29: Archidea Photo/Shutterstock; p.29 (LO): Phant/Shutterstock;
p.30: Irina K./Shutterstock; p.31 (UP): Levent Konuk/Shutterstock; p.31
(LO): Sogno Lucido/Shutterstock

Library and Archives Canada Cataloguing in Publication

Christopher, Clara, author
        Animal jokes, riddles, and games / Clara Christopher.

(No kidding!)
Includes index.
Issued in print and electronic formats.
ISBN 978-0-7787-2387-5 (bound).--
ISBN 978-0-7787-2391-2 (paperback).--
ISBN 978-1-4271-1744-1 (html)

        1. Animals--Juvenile humor. 2. Wit and humor, Juvenile.
3. Riddles, Juvenile. I. Title.

PN6231.A5C57 2016   jC818'.602   C2015-907474-6
                                           C2015-907475-4

Library of Congress Cataloging-in-Publication Data

Names: Christopher, Clara, author.
Title: Animal jokes, riddles, and games / Clara Christopher.
Description: New York ; Crabtree Publishing Company, 2016. | Series:
    No kidding! | Includes index.
Identifiers: LCCN 2016002785 (print) | LCCN 2016006083 (ebook) |
    ISBN 9780778723875 (reinforced library binding : alk. paper) |
    ISBN 9780778723912 (pbk. : alk. paper) |
    ISBN 9781427117441 (electronic HTML)
Subjects: LCSH: Animals--Juvenile humor. | Wit and humor, Juvenile.
Classification: LCC PN6231.A5 C53 2016 (print) | LCC PN6231.A5
    (ebook) | DDC 808.88/2--dc23
LC record available at http://lccn.loc.gov/2016002785

Crabtree Publishing Company
www.crabtreebooks.com   1-800-387-7650

Printed in Canada/032016/EF20160210

Published in Canada
Crabtree Publishing
616 Welland Ave.
St. Catharines, Ontario
L2M 5V6

Published in the United States
Crabtree Publishing
PMB 59051
350 Fifth Avenue, 59th Floor
New York, New York 10118

Published in the United Kingdom
Crabtree Publishing
Maritime House
Basin Road North, Hove
BN41 1WR

Published in Australia
Crabtree Publishing
3 Charles Street
Coburg North
VIC, 3058

Contents

Chapter 1
Are You Kitten Me?

Why do we laugh when baby panda bears tumble to the ground, or when dogs excitedly run laps around a living room or a park? What is it about animals that we find so funny? Sometimes, we find it funny when animals act in ways that, to us, seem silly or clumsy. Sometimes it's an animal's physical appearance that seems funny, and we smile at things such as a donkey's teeth or the googley-eyes of a fish. We also laugh when animals behave in ways that seem human, such as a cat sitting upright, as a person would.

ANTHROPO-WHAT?

Look around you. Almost every animal movie, book, joke, or cartoon features animals with human traits. And humor is one of those traits. Think of Bugs Bunny. He's a cartoon rabbit who walks, talks, and cracks jokes. Giving an animal human qualities is called **anthropomorphism**. That's a big word, but it describes how animals, plants, or even objects are given human **characteristics** such as humor or anger. No rabbit can actually talk. And we don't know if rabbits laugh or smile. But if we put a rabbit in human clothing, or show the rabbit walking on two legs, we sure find it funny!

Pictures and videos of animals are especially funny when the animal seems to show human traits, such as the ability to talk.

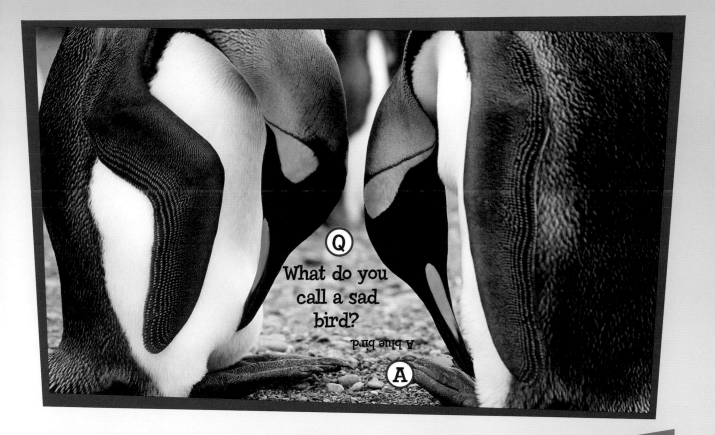

Q What do you call a sad bird?

A A blue bird.

Q Where do Dutch hamsters live?

A Hamsterdam!

FuNnY BoNe:

A farce is a type of comedy that features crazy or unlikely situations to make an audience laugh. Farces can be plays, movies, or works of literature. Physical humor, naughty jokes, and outrageous situations are common in farces. The word farce comes from the French word farcir, which means "to stuff (something) with."

THE OLD PLAY-ON-WORDS ROUTINE

While some humor is visual, other humor may be found in the way we use language. We often see jokes that use a "play on words." For example, check out this old joke:

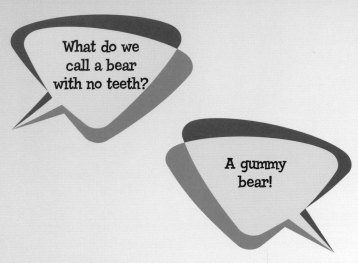

What do we call a bear with no teeth?

A gummy bear!

The answer, "gummy bear," contains a double meaning. One meaning refers to an actual description of a bear without teeth, and the other meaning refers to the yummy candy bears we eat!

ANATOMY OF A JOKE

A joke typically has two parts: the setup and the punch line. The setup provides the audience with background information. This background information sets the stage for the joke by building **expectations** of what is to follow. Once the audience reaches the punch line, however, they often realize that the setup information is misleading. That is, the information we are given to start with leads us to false expectations.

The punch line is the final statement of a joke that brings out the funny part, or the zinger. It presents the audience with an unexpected outcome. And the surprise is what makes it funny— whether it comes in a one-line answer or a long-winded story.

Q Why did the duck cross the road?

A It was the chicken's day off!

Q How do you know if there is a rhinoceros under your bed?

A Your head hits the ceiling!

Q Are leopards hard to spot?

A Nope, that's how they come.

FuNnY BoNe:

In Ancient Greece, theater comedies usually had a character called the Eiron. He was a comedic character that mocked a boastful character, called the Alazon, by downplaying his own abilities. If the Alazon said "I'm the strongest man in this town!," the Eiron might respond, while lifting a car, "I'm not very strong at all. I think I'm the weakest person I know."

7

Chapter 2
Just Joking Around

Humor comes in many forms. Wordplay, such as puns or riddles, is a clever use of words. You have to put your thinking cap on before you can giggle.

PUNS FOR FUNS

A pun is a form of wordplay that suggests two or more meanings associated with one word. Puns can either be words that have multiple meanings, or two words that sound the same but have different meanings.

UNRAVEL THE MEANING

Do you like solving puzzles? If yes, then riddles are for you! A riddle is a question or statement phrased so that its meaning must be unraveled or solved like a puzzle. Riddles have a long history. Many ancient cultures passed riddles down **orally**. Some wrote them down, and historians have even found them in ancient books. Riddles can be presented as one question, or a series of questions.

What do we call two fish that are in love?

Sole mates.

To really get the humor in the joke above, you have to get the pun. "Sole" is a kind of fish, and a "soul" is a person's spirit. "Soul mates" are two people who are meant for each other.

Q
Why is a turtle so strong?

A
Because it can carry its house on its back.

8

GAG ME!

Often, humor doesn't need a language at all. Physical comedy, such as slapstick, relies on **exaggerated** gestures and a good understanding of the world around you. Visual **gags**, or sight gags, are another way to show humor without words. They can be anything from images and sketch comedy, to plays and movies. The viewer's interpretation of what is going on gives sight gags their humor.

Everyone knows that dogs can't iron or clean the house—that's what makes this image so funny!

Q What is black, white, and red all over?

A A sunburned penguin.

FuNnY BoNe:

"Funny animal" is a style of cartoons and comics where the animals live life just like humans. In the cartoons, the animals talk like humans and walk on two legs— even when they are four-legged. Well-known funny animals include Snoopy from the Peanuts comic strip, Yogi Bear, Goofy, Mickey Mouse, Felix the Cat, and Woody Woodpecker, to name just a few.

JUST LIKE THE ORIGINAL (NOT)

Have you ever **imitated** a family member (even the family dog) for fun? You might have even said you were "spoofing" them. A spoof, or a send-up, is a form of parody. Parodies are when people do a humorously exaggerated imitation of someone else. Often, parodies are of musicians, singers, or actors with a certain **signature** style. The person doing the spoofing may be poking fun at the person, or making a comment on their work. For example, if you did a parody of Justin Bieber, you might style your hair like him or copy his dance moves, but with enough exaggeration to make it funny.

Got your Bieber duds on? A good parody requires you to know your subject well.

Q

Why don't they let pigs drive cars?

A Because they would turn into road hogs!

THE SCIENCE OF LAUGHTER

Admit it, sometimes you get the giggles. Sometimes, once you start laughing, you just can't stop. It's natural. No, really, laughter is the body's natural response to humor. It's good for you! Studies show that laughter boosts the **immune system** and helps fight disease. Laughter helps people relax and feel good. It also helps the heart work better by increasing blood flow. So go ahead and laugh. It's good for you!

LAUGHING IS CONTAGIOUS

Scientists know that laughter is **innate**, which means that it is built into us rather than something we learn to do. Laughter is also a social thing, and it can be contagious. Babies start smiling at about six weeks old, and laugh by the time they are three-and-a-half months old. Their laughter is often in response to an adult laughing with them. When we see others laugh, we usually can't help but laugh too.

Ha! Ha! Ha! Ha! Ha! Ha! Ha! Ha! Ha! Ha! Ha! Ha! Ha!

Our facial and neck muscles contract as we laugh, and sometimes we laugh so hard that it feels like we can't breathe.

FuNnY BoNe:

Why are things funnier when we're in a quiet library? When we are put in situations that call on us to behave seriously or responsibly, we find it much more difficult to hold back laughter. This is because we must exercise our willpower in order to behave properly, and willpower is a limited resource. The more willpower we exercise, the more lively our emotions and impulses become!

Q

Why did the bee get married?

Because he found his honey.

A

Chapter 3
Language of Humor

Why did the chicken cross the road? To get to the other side. This old riddle is often criticized for its lack of humor. What, though, was the original humor in the joke? We might expect there to be some special, meaningful reason for the chicken's road crossing, but there really isn't any. And that's exactly what makes the old riddle humorous.

BUT THAT'S ABSURD!

Sometimes, there aren't meaningful reasons to explain why things take place. The chicken crossing the road riddle uses **absurd** humor to make that point. It makes a joke about there being no obvious joke. When we say something is absurd, we mean it is unreasonable or even ridiculous. Absurd things are often used as examples in humor. One reason for this is that humor helps us sort through our feelings, even if those feelings are anger or sadness. Poking fun at absurd things, such as big hairy dogs wearing sweaters, makes us laugh, and laughter relieves stress.

FUNNY FOLK

You probably know a class clown. Maybe you are one! Some people have a talent for humor. But very few people make a living out of being funny. Comedians are professional laugh-makers. They write jokes and then share them in routines they call "stand up." Being a stand-up comedian is hard work. Some take comedy classes to learn how to tell jokes in front of a crowd. Comedians also write a lot. They write about what they observe around them. Most of the jokes comedians write don't make it into their stage acts. In fact, some say only half of their jokes are good enough for an audience!

FuNnY BoNe:

On the Internet, memes are clever ideas that are shown in images or videos. Image memes can often be funny, especially if they have ridiculous catchphrases. Funny animal memes are very popular. The famous "doge" meme, which shows a Shiba Inu dog making a face, was featured in a Swedish ad campaign.

13

IT'S LIKE THIS...

Many jokes use **similes** to convey humor. A simile is a figure of speech that compares two separate things in an interesting way. Similes use connecting words such as "like" or "as." When you say "I was sick as a dog," you are using a simile. Here's another one:

BEING FUNNY WITH SIMILES

How can similes convey humor? They can be funny if they create an element of surprise. That is, if similes communicate a message that is different from our expectations, we will find them amusing. When you say "Sam is as graceful as a gazelle," you mean she is light-footed and elegant. That's a nice compliment. But if you say "Sam is as graceful as a St. Bernard," the simile might make your friends chuckle. It's funny because St. Bernard dogs are big and lumbering—the exact opposite of something graceful!

I'm as hungry as a horse.

Q What kind of dreams do horses have?

A Night mares.

Q What do you call a dog with no legs?

A It doesn't matter, he won't come anyway.

FuNnY BoNe:

Gelotology is the study of laughter. The term comes from the Greek word, gelos, which means laughter. Gelotologists study the effects of laughter on the body and on the mind.

Chapter 4
Playing With Words

My brother is such a monkey! I'm going to put a bug in Mom's ear, and maybe I'll finally get my own room. Metaphors, such as "my brother is such a monkey," and idioms, such as "put a bug in Mom's ear," are figures of speech that help you paint pictures with words. They can be funny, too!

METAPHORS AND IDIOMS

Metaphors compare two unrelated things, such as brothers and monkeys, in order to **vividly** describe something or make a point. Unlike similes, metaphors don't use "like" or "as."

Idioms are figures of speech that have a different meaning from their **literal** meaning. For example, "put a bug in mom's ear" means to give her a hint about something you want.

Q

What do you get if you cross a fish with an elephant?

A

They get all wrapped up in their work! A-fish-ant. Get it?

Q Why are igloos round?

A So polar bears can't hide in the corners!

Q What happens when a frog's car breaks down?

A He gets toad away.

FuNnY BoNe:

Scooby-Doo is a mystery-solving Great Dane who has appeared in animated cartoons since 1969. Scooby can talk, and is known for hilariously adding an "r" to the beginning of most words. This turns "uh oh" into "ruh roh," and his own name into Rooby-Roo!

LANGUAGE AND MEANING

Metaphors and idioms deal with language that is literal, and meanings that are **figurative**, or meant to be a symbol instead of a fact. So when we say "it's really raining cats and dogs out there," we don't mean cats and dogs are literally falling from the sky. We mean the rain is ridiculously heavy. It would be silly to think cats and dogs could actually rain down from the sky...wouldn't it?

DOES NOT TRANSLATE

Idioms are unique to the language they come from. A German idiom might make sense in German, but probably not when translated into English. For example, the German idiom *schwein gehabt* means "having pig." It's a saying that has no equivalent in English, and it means to have luck. The idiom comes from the German custom of eating pork for dinner. Meat was costly, so those who could afford to eat it were considered lucky.

Q What did one flea say to the other flea?

A Shall we walk to the picnic, or take the dog?

Q What happens when a cat eats a lemon?

A It becomes a sour puss!

Q What time is it when an elephant sits on your fence?

A Time to get a new fence!

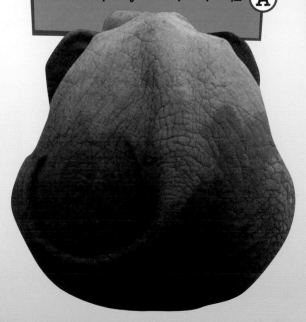

FuNnY BoNe:

Has anyone ever told you that you are witty? Wit is a kind of humor where a person makes funny and clever remarks, often as comebacks to something someone else has said. Wit is thought of as smart humor, because a person has to know about the world around them in order to quickly think of snappy replies.

Chapter 5
SOUNDS, AH, FAMILIAR

Sometimes we come across two words that mean the same thing. These words are called synonyms. We are also likely to come across homonyms, or words that sound similar but mean different things, and antonyms, or words that mean the exact opposite of others. In humor writing, as in any other kind of writing, it is handy to know your "nyms."

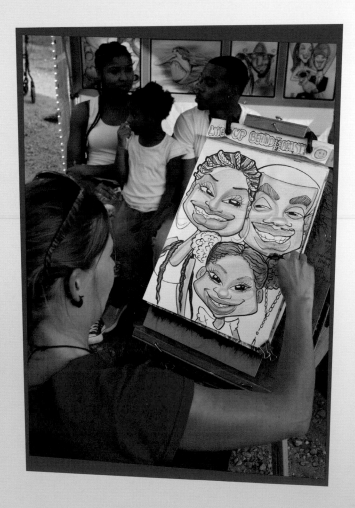

DOG, POOCH, CANINE

The word synonym comes from Ancient Greece. The **prefix** "syn" means "with," and the **suffix** "onym" means "name." Synonyms make for interesting writing. When crafting a joke, they can bring otherwise dull descriptions to vibrant life. A synonym for a dog is canine, but in a joke about a funny dog, you might use pooch, fur ball, tail-wagger, or even fleabag. Finding synonyms is easy if you have a thesaurus. A thesaurus is like a dictionary, except it only lists synonyms for words.

An artist draws caricatures of people on the street.

Q

Why did the turkey cross the road?

A

To prove he wasn't chicken!

Q

What animal has more lives than a cat?

A

Frogs, they croak every night!

Q

What is "out of bounds?"

A

An exhausted kangaroo!

FuNnY BoNe:

Most often, we think of caricatures as those exaggerated cartoons we see artists draw on the street. Caricatures are pictures, but they are also imitations of personality traits. Clowns and comics sometimes portray caricatures of well-known figures, such as actors or political leaders.

THE EXACT OPPOSITE

When two words have opposite meanings, we call those words antonyms. The word antonym also comes from Ancient Greece. In Greek, "anti" means against, and "onymon" means name. For example, an antonym for big would be little. Some animal-related antonyms include furry-smooth, sweet-vicious, loud-quiet, and fast-slow.

SAME SOUND, DIFFERENT MEANING

When is an ant also an aunt? When it's a homonym! Mastering homonyms can make you feel like you are king of the castle. They are words that sound the same or are spelled the same but have different meanings. For example, ant means the insect, while aunt is your relative. It is easy to mistake one for the other, which can also be funny. For example, if you were writing a joke about dog "chews" and used the word "choose" instead. Get it? Chews are a type of dog treat, while choose is a word that means select.

SAME BUT NOT THE SAME

Homophones are words that sound the same, but have different spellings and meanings. For example: deer (the animal) and dear (what your grandma might call you), or gorilla (the animal) and guerrilla (the fighting method).

Q Why are teddy bears never hungry?

A They are always stuffed!

This dog chooses to chew his bone. Knowing your "nyms" can be a slobbering good time!

Q What did the farmer call the cow that had no milk?

A An udder failure.

Q What kind of wagon does a dog have?

A A tail waggin'!

Q Why are fish so smart?

A Because they live in schools.

23

Chapter 6
Animal Fun and Games

Humans may not be the only species that laughs. A number of other animals are believed to yuck it up, too. Scientists studied rats while being tickled and then recorded the results. The rats made chirping noises exactly like they did when they were playing! Similar tickle experiments on gorillas and chimpanzees showed they can laugh, too.

Q

Why do gorillas have big nostrils?

Because they have big fingers!

A

KOKO CRACK JOKE?

Koko the gorilla knows more than 2,000 words in **American Sign Language**. Apparently, when asked "What can you think of that is hard?" Koko has signed both "rock" and "work." Koko's handlers believe this shows that not only was Koko able to understand the question, she also understood its different meanings.

It also shows that Koko may have been cracking her version of a joke, by expressing her own dislike for working! The handlers also believe Koko can smile and laugh.

LOOK AT THAT DOG LAUGH!

Ask a dog owner if they think their dog smiles and their answer will probably be "yes!" Some animal **behaviorists** believe dogs can laugh, but it just sounds different from human laughing. They studied dogs and found that they make a forced heavy breathing sound when having fun or at play. When other dogs hear this sound—even as a recording—they bow with their front legs lowered as an **invitation** to play.

Q Why are elephants so wrinkly?

A Because it takes so long to iron them.

Q Where did the tail-less dog go to shop?

A To the retail store.

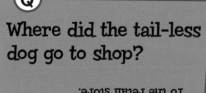

FuNnY BoNe:

Guffaw, giggle, chortle, titter, chuckle, and snicker...there are many synonyms for the word laughter. Here is one new one to try: cachinnate. It comes from the Latin word cachinnatus, which means to laugh aloud or uncontrollably. Mirth is a also a word for laughter that is rarely used today. It is of Germanic origin, and means amusement expressed in laughter. Try using them in a sentence!

MAKE YOUR OWN COMIC STRIP

Comic strips are a visual way of telling a story or joke. Comics have a beginning, a middle, and an end, and each scene is shown in a panel. So let's get going! Grab some paper and a pencil, draw a series of panels like the ones below, and follow the instructions below to create your own comic strip.

1. **The Setting:** Use your first panel to show where the story happens. Is it in a classroom, a playground, your own home, or on the street?

2. **The Main Characters:** Add a close-up of one or more of the main characters, either in an action scene or speaking.

3. **All Characters:** Move the story along by adding more characters.

4. **The Ending:** You can end the comic here, or you can continue the comic with a cliffhanger and a "to be continued."

Tips:

- Adding sound effects such as "eep" and "whoosh," along with movement lines, will make your comic more action-oriented.

- Make your comic funny by drawing characters showing emotion. You don't have to draw an entire body. Think of just drawing faces that look angry or sad.

- Draw big when you can. Remember that you can copy the panels and practice your skills over and over again.

- Use symbols such as light bulbs or thought bubbles to show what a character is thinking.

- Practice makes perfect. Draw with a pencil, erase what doesn't work, and trace over the parts you want to keep.

FuNnY BoNe:

"See you in the funny papers" is an old way of saying goodbye. The saying comes from a time when newspapers printed special color comic strip sections in Sunday papers. Originally, it wasn't meant as something nice to say. It was meant as an insult, as if to say "you are odd or strange, like the comics." Now it just means "see ya later."

Chapter 7
Your Guide to Funny

Think of a friend or family member you find funny. What is it that makes him or her funny? What tricks of the trade do they use? How can you hone your own funny bone? Here are some tips:

1. **Be a good listener:** To be funny, you have to know your audience and what they like and dislike. Ask yourself "what kind of humor will this audience appreciate?" People have wide ranging senses of humor, and it takes getting to know the crowd you're joking with to make your comedy routine successful.

2. **Learn to "read a room":** Sometimes people think they are kidding around, but their jokes fall flat. Comedians and jokesters are keen observers of their surroundings. They know that if one joke doesn't get a laugh, they shouldn't hammer it senseless. If your friend isn't laughing at your joke, it may be because something else is bothering them. Check your humor and read the room, and adjust your behavior to match.

3. **Understand timing:** All humor requires timing. If you rush a joke or a story, your audience may miss the **punch line**. Learn to emphasize one or more parts of your joke, using pauses in-between to create tension. That tension will make the punch line funnier.

4. **Stay true to yourself:** One important part of being funny is understanding your own personal sense of humor. Not everyone will find your humor funny, but when others sense that you are speaking and acting like the real you, they might appreciate how you see things.

5. **Be humble:** Everyone appreciates people who can make fun of themselves—and who can joke about others without being hurtful.

HEE HAW!

Got a funny picture of your family pet? Try your hand at making your own meme or animal comic. If you don't have a pet, try it with an old magazine photo, or print an image of an animal from the Internet. But first, ask your parent if you can print or cut the image. Paste the image on a sheet where you have drawn a comic panel. Add a speech bubble or thought bubble. Add what you think the animal is thinking or saying in the bubble. You can even make a cartoon, or a pictoon, by drawing details around the photo.

Q What kind of dog is always cold?

A A chill dog.

Knock, knock.

Who's there?

Who.

Who who?

FuNnY BoNe:

Situational humor is the kind of yucks that arise from daily life. It makes humor out of odd or unexpected events that happen in day-to-day activities. You may have heard the abbreviated term "sitcom" before to describe a type of television show. This term stands for situational comedy. Some sitcoms are filmed in front of live audiences so that you can hear the audience laugh at the humor. Others feature laugh tracks, or taped laughing, that is used after punch lines are delivered.

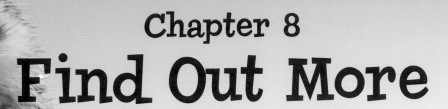

Chapter 8
Find Out More

Looking for a hee-hawing good time?
Check out these resources for added fun.

BOOKS:

Barry, Dave. *The Worst Class Trip Ever*. Disney-Hyperion, 2015.

Leno, Jay. *How to Be the Funniest Kid in the Whole Wide World*. Simon & Schuster, 2005.

National Geographic Kids. *Funny Animals! Collection: Amazing Stories of Hilarious Animals and Surprising Talents*. National Geographic Children's Books, 2015.

MUSEUMS:

Many children's museums feature fun and funny exhibits that encourage kids to develop their sense of humor.

- Please Touch Museum. Philadelphia, PA
  www.pleasetouchmuseum.org
- Children's Museum of Houston. Houston, TX
  www.cmhouston.org
- The Ontario Science Centre, Toronto, ON
  www.ontariosciencecentre.ca

Hall of Humor

Chewbacca

Okay, he's not a real animal. In fact, Chewbacca is a Wookie, an alien species in the *Star Wars* movie series. His character, Han Solo's co-pilot, was created based on orangutan behavior. Chewie, as he is nicknamed, is like most animals in comedies—a sidekick. He plays the **eccentric** to Han Solo, who acts frustrated by his behavior.

Mister Ed

Hollywood loves a good animal comedy, and because of that there are many famous animal actors. But very few animal actors made an impact like Mister Ed. This "talking" horse had his own television show in the 1950s! Bamboo Harvester, a **palomino**, played Mister Ed. In the show, Mister Ed moves his lips when talking. Producers originally did this by placing a nylon thread in his mouth and pulling it. Bamboo Harvester learned how to move his lips by himself, without the thread. That's one smart horsie!

Glossary

Note: Some boldfaced terms are defined where they appear in the text

absurd Humor that seems foolish or not reasonable

American Sign Language A form of sign language used in the United States and Canada. It is a method for deaf people to communicate using hand signs.

anthropomorphism Giving human characteristics or behavior to something that is not human

behaviorist A scientist who studies and explains animal or human behavior

characteristics A feature or quality of a person

eccentric A person, animal, or thing that does not follow conventional or accepted conduct

expectation A belief in something

exaggerated To describe something as larger, greater, or better than it really is

figurative Describing something symbolic or metaphorical, that is not meant to be taken as fact

gags A type of practical humor without words

immune system The body's system for staying healthy and fighting disease

imitated To copy something or someone, especially for comic effect

invitation A request that is written, spoken, or in the case of an animal, expressed through behavior

literal A true or actual meaning

orally Something that is spoken, sung, or said

palomino A pale-golden or tan-colored horse with a white mane or tail

prefix A word or letter placed at the beginning of a word to change its meaning

punch line A sentence, statement, or action in comedy that drives home the point of the joke

signature A special or distinct feature or characteristic by which someone can be identified, such as a signature way of dressing

suffix Letters placed at the end of a word to make another form of that word, for example: run and running

vividly Something powerfully or clearly described

Index